NORTH & SOUTH AMERICA

Coastlines and Land Bridges

Contir

Bruce McClish

www.heinemann.co.uk/library

Visit our website to find out more information about Heinemann Library books.

To order:

☎ Phone 44 (0) 1865 888066

▤ Send a fax to 44 (0) 1865 314091

▢ Visit the Heinemann Bookshop at www.heinemann.co.uk/library to browse our catalogue and order online.

First published 2003 in Austrailia by Heinemann Library a division of Harcourt Education Australia, 18–22 Salmon Street, Port Melbourne Victoria 3207 Australia (a division of Reed International Books Australia Pty Ltd, ABN 70 001 002 357).

© Reed International Books Australia Pty Ltd 2003
First published in paperback in 2005.
The moral right of the proprietor has been asserted.

Editor: Carmel Heron
Designer: Stella Vassiliou
Photo researcher: Margaret Maher
Production controller: Chris Roberts
Maps and diagrams by Pat Kermode and Stella Vassiliou

Film separations by Digital Imaging Group (DIG), Melbourne, Australia
Printed in China by WKT Company Ltd.

ISBN 1 74070 128 3 (hardback)
07 06 05 04 03
10 9 8 7 6 5 4 3 2 1

ISBN 0 431 18163 2 (paperback)
09 08 07 06 05
10 9 8 7 6 5 4 3 2 1

British Library of Cataloguing in Publication Data
McClish, Bruce.
North & South America: New world continents & land bridges - (All About Continents)
917
A full catalogue record for this book is available from the British Library.

Acknowledgements

The author would like to thank: Avi Olshina, geologist, Victorian Government; Peter Nunan, geography teacher, Royal Geographical Society of Queensland; Craig Campbell, researcher; Jenny McClish, researcher and contributing author.

Main cover images of Death Valley, California, and market in Ecuador supplied by PhotoDisc.

Other images supplied by: ANT Photo Library/Pavel German: p. 22; Australian Picture Library/Corbis © Jay Dickman: pp. 16 (right), 25, /© Kevin Fleming: p. 29, /© Philip Gould: p. 5 (bottom), /© Wolfgang Kaehler: p. 16 (left), /© Danny Lehman: pp. 13, 21, /© Marko Modic: p. 17, /© NASA: p. 5 (top), /© Fulvio Roiter: p. 15 (bottom), /© Joseph Sohm: p. 12, /© Nik Wheeler: p. 19; AUSCAPE/Francois Gohier: p. 15 (top); PhotoDisc: pp. 7, 8, 9, 10, 11, 18, 27.

Contents

THE AMERICAS

A continent is a huge **landmass** on the surface of the Earth. We generally speak of seven continents: Europe, Asia, Africa, North America, South America, Australia and Antarctica. Some continents are quite unlike one another, such as Europe and Africa or Asia and Antarctica. Continents such as these have big differences in shape, size, climate, plants, animals and human cultures.

On the other hand, some continents have many traits in common, and are often associated with each other. North America and South America are two such continents. They are the only continents that share the same name, and are even grouped together as the Americas. They are also known as 'New World' continents. This is not because the Americas are younger than the other continents. It is because the people who named the Americas were from Europe, and European civilisation came to North and South America much later than it did to the 'Old World' continents of Europe, Asia and Africa.

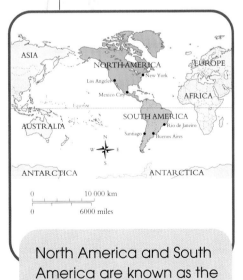

North America and South America are known as the New World continents.

New World links

There are very good reasons for grouping North America with South America. The two continents are linked by the narrow **Isthmus** of Panama. North America and South America each have great mountain ranges on their western sides and great lowland regions on their eastern sides. They share many kinds of animals, such as armadillos, **peccaries**, **opossums**, jaguars, pumas and vampire bats. They also have similarities in human culture, such as the Spanish language and the Roman Catholic religion, which are common on both continents.

Central America is a narrow area of land between Mexico and South America. Central America, and the seven countries in it, is often referred to as a region on its own. But Central America is not a separate continent. It is part of North America.

A much wider area, shared by both continents, is called Latin America. All of the Americas south of the USA – including Mexico, Central America and South America – forms Latin America. In this region, most people speak Spanish (or Portuguese) and belong to the Roman Catholic religion.

Land bridges

The Isthmus of Panama is a land bridge – an area of land that connects two continents. A land bridge makes it easier for plants, animals and people to cross over into different continents. Land bridges are not always permanent; they often change, disappear or reappear over a period of time. For example, the land bridge formed by the Isthmus of Panama did not exist more than three million years ago. Land bridges can also be a variety of shapes and sizes. Dozens of land bridges have linked different continents over billions of years. Understanding land bridges, past and present, helps us understand the wildlife and human culture of continents.

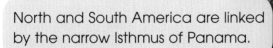

North and South America are linked by the narrow Isthmus of Panama.

Blessing of the Tombs ceremony on All Saints Day, Louisiana, USA. The Roman Catholic religion is practised in North and South America.

Introducing
NORTH AMERICA

North America is the third-largest continent. Only Africa and Asia are larger. No other continent has a wider variety of landforms and climates – including **polar** mountains, **fertile** plains, scorched deserts, **tropical** beaches and lush green forests.

The name 'North America' does not mean the same thing as America. The name 'America' can mean any part of North or South America. But when many people say 'America', they simply mean 'the USA' (the United States of America). Of course, the continent of North America is much larger than the USA, and includes more than 15 other countries. (One of these countries, Canada, is actually larger than the USA.) Most North American countries are small, and lie in Central America, a region that forms the narrow tropical tip of the continent. Many islands are also considered part of North America, including Greenland, Cuba and Jamaica.

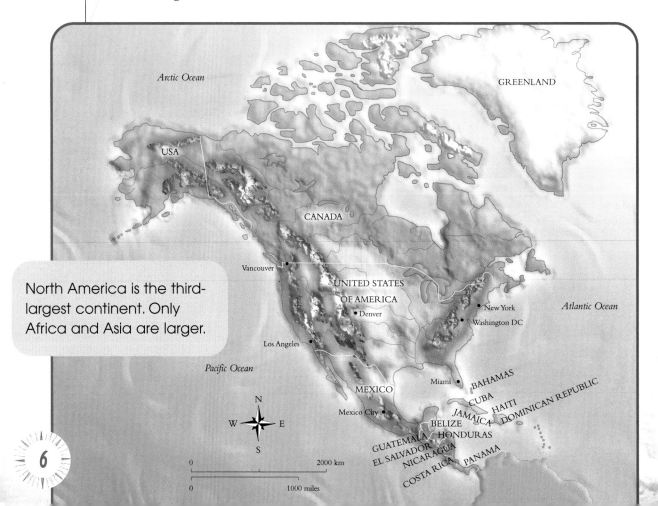

North America is the third-largest continent. Only Africa and Asia are larger.

Area: 24 400 000 sq km

Climate: mainly **temperate**, with some large polar and tropical regions

Population: 495 369 000 (estimated 2002)

Biggest country: Canada (9 976 140 sq km)

Highest peak: Mt McKinley (6194 metres above sea level)

Lowest point: Death Valley, California (86 metres below sea level)

Largest freshwater lake: Lake Superior (82 400 sq km)

Longest river: Missouri River (4320 km)

Biggest desert: Greenland (2 175 600 sq km)

Crop products: wheat, corn, oats, rice, cotton, soya beans, flaxseed, **sorghum**, citrus fruits, bananas, potatoes, coffee, sugar cane, tobacco

Animals and animal products: cattle (beef and dairy), pigs, sheep, chickens, eggs, fish

Mineral products: coal, petroleum, natural gas, uranium, gold, silver, nickel, copper, zinc, lead, iron ore, phosphate, molybdenum

Manufactured products: automobiles and automobile parts, electronic equipment, aircraft, chemicals, iron and steel, cement, fertiliser, paper products

North America has the world's largest island (Greenland), largest freshwater lake (Lake Superior) and tallest tree (California redwood). It is the wealthiest continent, rich in **natural resources** such as water, soil, timber and minerals. With growing businesses and industries, millions of North Americans enjoy the world's highest **standard of living**.

The Death Valley desert has the lowest point in North America.

Landforms

North America is shaped roughly like a giant triangle. The western part of the continent has the highest mountains and the driest deserts. The eastern part has lower mountains, bigger lakes and wider plains. The northern side of the continent is the coldest, and is cut by a great number of bays and inlets.

Mountains and deserts

The Rocky Mountains ('the Rockies') are North America's largest mountain range. They reach from Alaska in the north all the way down to Mexico in the south. The eastern side of the Rockies rises sharply, forming a great wall overlooking the neighbouring plains. The Sierra Nevada of California and the Sierra Madre of Mexico are other significant ranges. Many large desert regions lie between North America's western ranges.

The Grand Tetons. The western part of North America has the highest mountains.

The Appalachian Mountains are one of the few great ranges on the eastern side of North America. These mountains are older and more worn down than the western mountains. North American mountains have been a major source of mineral wealth, including gold, silver and coal.

East of the Rockies lie North America's great inland plains, or prairie regions. These include a vast region of ranches and farmlands stretching for hundreds of kilometres across the middle of the continent. More **fertile** lowlands are found closer to the east coast. The ancient, rocky north-eastern part of the continent also has many low-lying regions. The land has mineral wealth, but is poor for farming. This region is known as the Canadian Shield. (A shield is the **exposed** core of a continent and it contains very ancient rocks.)

Waterways

Many of North America's low-lying regions were worn down by giant **glaciers** of the last **ice age**. These glaciers also formed basins for the continent's biggest lakes. The Great Lakes, lying between Canada and the USA, cover an area almost as big as New Zealand. The Great Lakes region, and all the waterways that connect it to the sea, forms one of the main business and industrial centres of North America.

East of the Rockies and across the wide lowlands is where North America's longest rivers flow, including the Mississippi and the Missouri rivers. West of the Rockies, rivers are more likely to flow through spectacular gorges and canyons. The Yukon, Fraser, Mackenzie, Columbia, Colorado, Snake and Rio Grande are some of North America's western rivers.

Diary of a continent

▶ **300 million years ago:**
Coal-age swamps cover much of the continent.

▶ **250 million years ago:**
North America is part of the Laurasian supercontinent, along with Europe and Asia.

▶ **100 million years ago:**
A great sea floods the middle of the continent, dividing it into two **landmasses**.

▶ **95–65 million years ago:**
The Rocky Mountains begin to uplift.

▶ **2 million years ago:**
Ice-age glaciers cover much of the continent.

▶ **30 000–15 000 years ago:**
Humans enter North America from Asia (across Bering land bridge).

The Colorado River shaped the deep gorges of the Grand Canyon over millions of years.

Climate, plants and animals

A temperate climate

North America has every kind of climate, from frozen **polar** lands to steamy tropics. Most of the continent is in the **temperate** zone, where it never remains too hot or too cold. Although North America has lots of rainfall, it does have some large desert regions. The western deserts can be very hot in the day, but very cold at night, especially during the winter months. Even colder are the polar deserts of the continent's arctic north. Polar deserts are covered with little more than ice, snow or rock and they have very low rainfall.

Forests

North America's temperate regions are ideal for the growth of forests. Common trees are evergreen **conifers** (such as pine, fir and cedar) and

broad-leaved **deciduous trees** (such as oak, maple and hickory). North America also has rainforests, in tropical Central America. Huge areas of the continent's forests still remain standing in national parks and other reserves that are protected from logging.

North America has some of the world's tallest desert plants.

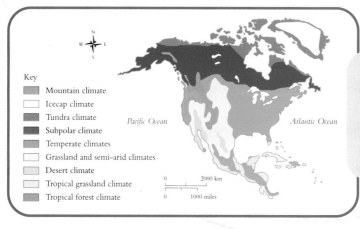

Key
- Mountain climate
- Icecap climate
- Tundra climate
- Subpolar climate
- Temperate climates
- Grassland and semi-arid climates
- Desert climate
- Tropical grassland climate
- Tropical forest climate

Pacific Ocean   *Atlantic Ocean*

0   2000 km

0   1000 miles

Although North America is mainly temperate, it has every kind of climate, from steamy tropics to polar **icecaps**.

Grasslands

Just as important as forests are the immense grassland regions, especially on the inland plains of North America. Some native grasses of North America can grow taller than a person. Most of the grassland regions are now used for ranching or farming.

Wildlife

North America has many animals that are similar to those of the nearest continents. In its northern regions it has elk, caribou, wild sheep, bears, foxes and hares similar to those of Europe and North Asia. In its southern regions, it has armadillos, jaguars, monkeys and parrots similar to those of South America. Yet North America has some unique animals, such as the coyote and the **pronghorn**, which are found nowhere else in the world. Some of the continent's animals, such as the bison and the bald eagle, have been seriously threatened by hunting and land clearing over the past two centuries. Fortunately, many of these animals are now protected in special parks and reserves.

Animals and habitats

Temperate forests
- brown bear
- North American black bear
- wolf
- lynx
- wolverine
- mink
- white-tailed deer
- moose
- raccoon
- skunk
- beaver
- muskrat
- porcupine
- red squirrel

Deserts
- bobcat
- kangaroo rat
- sidewinder rattlesnake
- jackrabbit
- peccary
- chuckwalla
- tortoise
- elf owl
- gila monster
- roadrunner

Mountains
- puma
- Rocky Mountain goat
- bighorn sheep
- Dall sheep

Grasslands
- coyote
- bison
- pronghorn
- mule deer
- prairie dog
- pocketgopher
- prairie falcon
- prairie chicken
- rattlesnake

Tropical Central America
- spidermonkey
- howler monkey
- jaguar
- coati
- kinkajou
- peccary

Polar regions
- polar bear
- wolf
- seal
- caribou
- musk ox
- snowy owl

North American forests are often a mixture of conifers and deciduous trees. These temperate forests are an important habitat for many animals.

History and culture

The first people who entered North America came from prehistoric Asia, thousands of years ago. They became known as Native Americans (also called American Indians) and Inuits (or Eskimos). Some of their groups settled in one place, in villages, farms or cities. Others were more nomadic, travelling from camp to camp, hunting and gathering food in different places.

Europeans take over

Vikings from Europe began exploring North America around AD 1000. By the 1500s, Europeans from Spain, France and England were exploring and settling the 'new' continent. Many were trying to seize all the land or precious minerals they could get hold of. But some came simply because they were tired of living under the harsh laws of European rulers. Europeans spread rapidly throughout the continent, bringing their languages, religions and customs wherever they went.

Fighting often broke out between Native Americans and Europeans, or between the different European groups. Sometimes Native Americans were forced to work as slaves. Black Africans were also brought in as slaves. Today, slavery is illegal, and relations are normally peaceful among the different groups.

North Americans can be very loyal to their own country. Although their culture is still European, they like to be known as citizens of their North American country (such as 'Mexicans' or 'Canadians'). These countries are now independent, no longer ruled by a European government.

Most people of Anglo–America speak English and have a high standard of living.

Cultural regions

North America has two main cultural regions. One region is called Anglo-America, and it is made up of the USA and Canada. Most people in Anglo-America speak English, and have a high **standard of living**. Families of Anglo-America are not as closely tied as they are in the rest of the Americas. When children grow up, many are willing to live and work hundreds of kilometres away from their parents, brothers and sisters.

The other region is called Middle America. It is made up of Mexico, Central America and many nearby islands. Most people here speak Spanish and their culture is similar to that in South America. Although the standard of living is not as high as in Anglo-America, the families are much closer.

A Mexican market. Most people in Middle America have a Latin American culture, similar to that of South America.

Facts about living in **North America**

- Most North Americans have ancestors who were Native Americans, Europeans or Africans – or a mixture of these groups.

- **Christianity** and **Judaism** are the main religions of North America. Catholicism is one of the main Christian groups, especially in Middle America and Canada.

- North America manufactures more products than any other continent, except Europe.

- The USA and Canada have one of the most highly developed transportation and communication systems in the world.

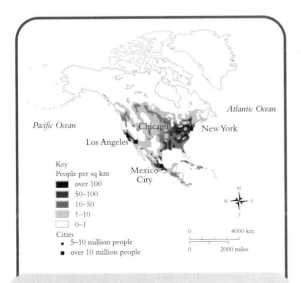

Key
People per sq km
- over 100
- 50–100
- 10–50
- 1–10
- 0–1

Cities
- 5–10 million people
- over 10 million people

Pacific Ocean
Atlantic Ocean
Chicago
New York
Los Angeles
Mexico City

0   4000 km
0   2000 miles

North America has the fourth-largest population of the continents.

Introducing
SOUTH AMERICA

South America is the fourth-largest continent. It forms the largest part of Latin America, that region of the Americas where most people speak Spanish or Portuguese. The continent is almost completely surrounded by seas, linked with North America only by the narrow **Isthmus** of Panama.

South America is a continent of extreme contrasts. It is a land where snowy peaks stand near **tropical** rainforests, parched deserts or cold, wind-swept islands. It is also a land of extremely rich people and extremely poor people, where modern cities contrast with tiny Indian villages. Most of South America is not densely populated. Although the continent is more than double the size of Europe, its population is much smaller.

South America has the world's largest rainforest (the Amazon Basin), longest mountain chain (the Andes Mountains), tallest waterfall (Salto Angel, also known as Angel Falls) and one of the driest deserts (the Atacama Desert). South America has great **natural resources**, including water, soil, **timber** and minerals. Most of these resources are not highly developed. The people have many problems to deal with, especially poverty and unstable government.

Caracas
VENEZUELA
GUYANA
SURINAM
FRENCH GUIANA
COLOMBIA
ECUADOR
Atlantic Ocean
BRAZIL
Lima
PERU
BOLIVIA
Pacific Ocean
PARAGUAY
CHILE
URUGUAY
Santiago
Buenos Aires
ARGENTINA

N
W — E
S

0   5000 km

0   3000 miles

South America is the fourth-largest continent.

South America:
facts and figures

Area: 17 864 000 sq km

Climate: tropical and **temperate**, with large areas of mountain and rainforest

Population: 355 418 000 (estimated 2002)

Biggest country: Brazil (8 511 965 sq km)

Highest peak: Mt Aconcagua (6960 metres)

Lowest point: Peninsula Valdés (40 metres below sea level)

Largest freshwater lake: Lake Titicaca (8300 sq km)

Longest river: Amazon River (6500 km)

Biggest desert: Patagonian Desert, Argentina (673 000 sq km)

Crop products: coffee, cocoa, cotton, soya beans, sugar, bananas, oranges, corn, wheat, timber, Brazil nuts, rubber

Animals and animal products: beef cattle, sheep, wool, fish and fish products

Mineral products: petroleum and petroleum products, natural gas, coal, molybdenum, bauxite, copper, tin, silver, gold, iron ore, zinc, lead, manganese, gemstones

Manufactured products: chemicals, processed foods, clothing and textiles, motor vehicles, aircraft, electronic equipment, furniture, weapons

Salto Angel Falls in Venezuela is the tallest waterfall in the world (979 metres).

South American cowboys called gauchos tend cattle on the plains of Argentina.

Landforms

Like North America, South America is shaped like a giant triangle. The western side of South America also has the highest mountains and driest deserts, with lower mountains and plains to the east. The **tropical** northern coast of South America is where some of the continent's biggest rivers drain into the sea, including the Amazon. The great landforms of South America are difficult to cross, often causing different communities to be isolated.

Mountains

The Andes Mountains are a great S-shaped chain of mountains on the western side of South America. The Andes curve more than 7000 kilometres along the edge of the continent, from the far tropical north all the way down to the cold southern tip. The Andes are 10–15 million years old and are still being shaped by volcanoes and **glaciers**. Only the Himalayas of Asia are higher. People of the Andes live on the slopes and in the many valleys and high plains between the peaks. Cities of this region are among the highest in the world. Other highland regions lie in the eastern part of South America. These are older and more worn down than the Andes.

The southern Andes is one of the coldest and stormiest regions of South America.

South American rivers provide important transportation routes in areas where roads are difficult to make.

Lowlands

Most of South America is made up of lowland regions, such as rolling hills and broad river valleys. Some of the lowlands are covered with dense rainforest, while others support only small trees, scrub or grass. One of the most **fertile** plains is the Pampas (or Pampa) region in the south-east. The Pampas is almost completely flat, with rich grasslands that are ideal for grazing beef cattle.

Rivers and rainforest

The Amazon River is the second-longest river in the world. It begins high in the Andes Mountains, fed by hundreds of mountain streams. From the far-western mountains it flows across a low tropical rainforest, all the way across to the Atlantic coast. Along its course, the Amazon picks up and carries more water than any other river in the world. It pours so many billions of litres into the Atlantic that the ocean water turns a muddy yellow colour, even hundreds of kilometres from the coast. Other major South American rivers include the Orinoco, Parana, Paraguay, São Francisco, Negro and Uruguay.

Diary of a continent

▶ **200 million years ago**
South America is part of the Gondwana supercontinent, along with Africa, Australia and Antarctica.

▶ **150 million years ago**
Gondwana breaks up.

▶ **45 million years ago**
South America is an island continent, cut off from all the others.

▶ **10–15 million years ago**
The Andes Mountains begin to uplift.

▶ **3 million years ago**
North America and South America are connected by the **Isthmus** of Panama.

▶ **2 million–10 000 years ago**
Ice-age glaciers cover the southern tip of Chile and Argentina.

▶ **30 000–12 000 years ago**
Humans enter North and South America from Asia on the Bering land bridge.

The driest deserts of South America lie on the western side of the Andes – although there are large **arid** regions on the south-eastern tip of the continent.

Climate, plants and animals

The largest part of South America lies in the tropics. This means that most of the continent has warm to hot weather throughout the year, usually with plenty of rain. About a third of the continent is covered with **tropical** rainforests. More than 2000 different kinds of trees live in these forests, along with many other native plants and animals.

Forests in danger

Rainforest plants are a valuable resource for **timber**, chemicals, medicine and food. The green leaves of rainforest plants produce large amounts of oxygen, which improves the quality of the Earth's air. Yet huge areas of rainforest are being cleared away, so the land can be used for ranches or farms. When the thick vegetation is cleared, there is little to protect the land from heavy rains, and much of the valuable soil is washed away. The land can only be saved by re-planting trees.

The temperate zone

Not all of South America is warm and rainy. Its high peaks are mainly cold and its deserts are mainly dry, even those in the tropical zone. South America is very long, and its narrow southern tip reaches far into the cooler **temperate** zone. This region lies closer to Antarctica than any other continent – less than a thousand kilometres away. (South America is often used as a base for Antarctic tours and expeditions.)

Equator

Pacific Ocean

Atlantic Ocean

N
W E
S

Key
Mountain climate
Tundra climate
Temperate climates
Grassland and semi-arid climates
Desert climate
Tropical grassland climate
Tropical forest climate

0   2000 km
0   1000 miles

The largest part of South America lies in the tropics. A narrow part of the continent reaches deep into the temperate zone.

Grasping claws and tails are features of many climbing rainforest animals.

Wildlife

A wide variety of animals live in South America. Some of these, such as the camel-like llamas and alpacas or the large rodents such as the **cavy** and **capybara**, are native only to this continent. The rainforest areas have the greatest variety of animals. Many of them are climbers – monkeys, **sloths**, **opossums** and **kinkajous** – with grasping claws or tails. On the ground are animals, such as **tapirs**, anteaters and army ants. Many rainforest animals, such as certain snakes, lizards and the water opossum, can both climb and swim. Amazon waters are home to **manatees**, catfish, lungfish, electric eels and the deadly piranha fish.

There are more kinds of birds in South America than in any other continent. A wide variety of colourful toucans, parrots and hummingbirds live in the tropics. The giant condor lives in the mountains and the ostrich-like rhea on the Pampas. Many seabirds live along the South American coast.

Islands
- Galapagos tortoise
- lava lizard
- marine iguana
- flightless cormorant
- tree finch
- ground finch

Grasslands and arid regions
- maned wolf
- Pampas fox
- tuco-tuco
- Pampas guinea pig
- mara
- Pampas deer
- giant anteater
- nine-banded armadillo
- fairy armadillo
- rhea
- burrowing owl

Mountains
- llama (domesticated)
- vicuña
- guanaco
- chinchilla
- condor
- Andean flamingo
- Chilean parakeet
- Darwin's frog

Tropical forests and rivers
- jaguar
- spider monkey
- howler monkey
- tapir
- sloth
- capybara
- vampire bat
- ocelot
- kinkajou
- coati
- woolly opossum
- water opossum
- paca
- peccary
- Amazon dolphin
- manatee
- toucan
- caiman (or cayman)
- anaconda
- poison arrow frog
- piranha

Llamas and alpacas are camel-like animals of the Andes Mountains. Mountain-dwelling people use these animals for carrying heavy loads and for wool.

History and culture

The first people to enter South America were Native Americans (American Indians). They came from North America thousands of years ago, crossing over on the **Isthmus** of Panama. They spread into all regions of the continent, from the **tropical** rainforest to the stormy southern tip. Many South American Indians hunted and gathered their food. Others farmed plants such as squash and beans. Some, such as the Incas, lived in large communities. The Incas ruled over a great empire in the Andes Mountains region, building temples, roads, bridges and irrigation systems. They also used pottery, metals, woven cloth and **domestic animals**.

European invasion

Europeans began arriving in South America during the 1500s. Most of them were from Spain or Portugal. They conquered the Indians they met up with, including the great Inca Empire. They began to settle the land, establishing mines and farms, and forcing the surviving Native Americans to work as slaves. More slaves were brought in from Africa. The Native Americans and Africans were later freed, but they remained much poorer than the Europeans. European settlements steadily grew into modern **nations**, such as Brazil, Peru, Bolivia and Chile. Many had to fight wars to gain their independence from European rule. Although South American countries are **democracies**, many have been taken over by **military dictators** in the past two centuries.

Isolation

Many regions of South America are still isolated from one another. Transport and communication have often been limited by the many natural barriers – mountains, deserts, swamps or rainforest – between the different regions. There are some roads and railways through these natural barriers, but many people still rely on animals, boats or aircraft to travel and communicate.

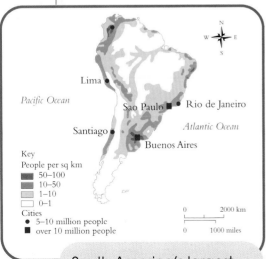

South America's largest population centres grew from European settlements.

Culture

South America is part of Latin America, with a similar culture to Central America. Most of the people speak Spanish or Portuguese. The people take great pride in their traditional art, craft, music and folklore. Families are very close, with parents, children, grandparents, uncles, aunts, cousins and other relatives living nearby or in the same house. Poverty is still a problem for many, even in the wealthier countries, such as Argentina, Brazil, Uruguay and Venezuela.

Facts about living in South America

- Like North Americans, most South Americans have ancestors who were Native Americans, Europeans or Africans – often a mixture of these groups.
- Most South Americans live in city areas. Some of the cities are very large, such as Caracas, Rio de Janeiro, São Paulo and Buenos Aires.
- Most towns and cities of South America lie on, or near, the coast.
- **Christianity** is the main religion in South America, with Catholicism practised by the largest group by far.

South Americans take great pride in their traditional arts and crafts.

21

Continental connections and
PLATE TECTONICS

As we know, North America and South America are joined together by a land bridge. This land bridge – the narrow **Isthmus** of Panama – allows plants, animals and people to **migrate** from one continent to the other. Without this connection, North and South America would be separated from each other, probably with very different kinds of wildlife and human cultures. Other land connections existed in ancient times. For example, North America was once connected with Europe, and South America was once connected with Africa.

Origin of land bridges

The Isthmus of Panama has existed for a long time, but it was not always there. Scientists believe it was formed around three million years ago. Before this time, North America and South America were separate continents, and had very different kinds of living things. So what caused the Isthmus of Panama to appear? What causes any land bridge to appear – or to disappear? These questions puzzled scientists for many years. They finally found the answers through the concept of plate **tectonics**.

False ideas

Before the mid-1900s, most people had a false idea about the continents. They believed that the continents stood motionless in the Earth, in the same place for billions of years. Yet, about 50 years ago, scientists discovered that the continents were moving. In fact, they have moved thousands of kilometres during ancient times, and are still moving today.

Mesosaurus was a crocodile-like reptile that once lived in South America and Africa 250 million years ago, when these two continents were joined.

Tectonic plates are made up of rock from the crust and the upper **mantle**. Each plate is about 100 kilometres thick. The rigid plates float on the next layer of rocks below, moving sideways along the hot lower surface. When the plates move, anything attached to them moves as well, including continents and parts of the ocean floor. This movement is very slow but the plates can cover long distances over millions of years.

Giant plates

Around the 1960s, scientists learned that the continents were attached to huge plates of rock, called tectonic plates. Together, the different plates make up the entire solid surface of the Earth, fitting together like a gigantic jigsaw puzzle. Many plates are larger than the continents, because they contain vast sections of the Earth's **crust**, including ocean floor. Despite their large size, tectonic plates move about over the Earth. They travel very slowly – about 10 centimetres every year – but they can cover great distances over millions of years. The idea of how plates move is called plate tectonics. Plate tectonics helps us understand the changing position of continents, and how land bridges are formed.

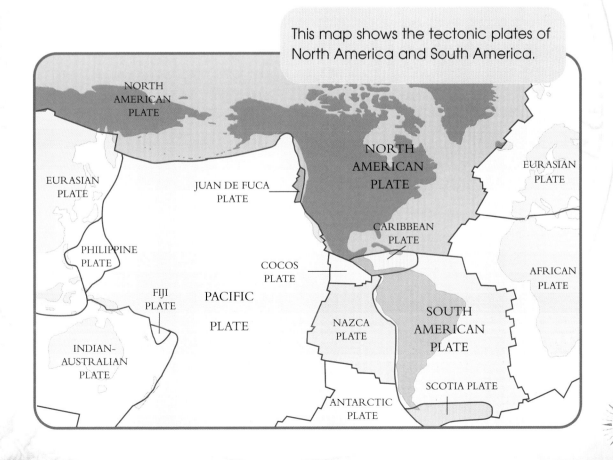

This map shows the tectonic plates of North America and South America.

NORTH AMERICAN PLATE

NORTH AMERICAN PLATE

EURASIAN PLATE

EURASIAN PLATE

JUAN DE FUCA PLATE

PHILIPPINE PLATE

COCOS PLATE

CARIBBEAN PLATE

AFRICAN PLATE

FIJI PLATE

PACIFIC PLATE

NAZCA PLATE

SOUTH AMERICAN PLATE

INDIAN-AUSTRALIAN PLATE

ANTARCTIC PLATE

SCOTIA PLATE

Plate **tectonics** helps us understand how the continents slowly move across the Earth's surface. When two continents get close enough, they are likely to form some kind of connection, such as a land bridge.

When we think of a land bridge, we are likely to picture a narrow neck of land – such as an **isthmus**. But there are also connecting areas that are much bigger and wider. In fact, sometimes two continents are pushed right up against each other, so that there is one continuous, connecting **landmass**. Europe is connected to Asia in this way. When continents form one landmass, they become one larger continent. (This is why Europe together with Asia is called Eurasia.)

Ancient supercontinents

Today, Europe and Asia are the only continents to be pushed together to form one continent. Yet we know that the tectonic plates have been drifting around the planet for billions of years, and all of the continents have been pushed together at one time or another. The enormous landmass, formed as the plates carried several continents together, is called a supercontinent.

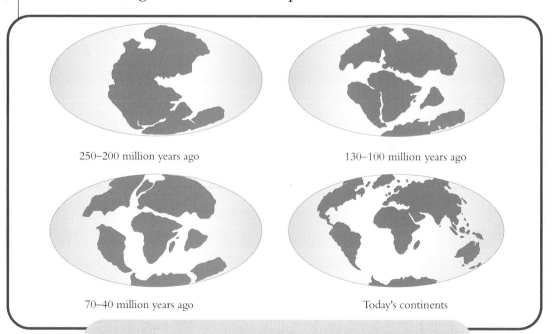

250–200 million years ago

130–100 million years ago

70–40 million years ago

Today's continents

The continents that once belonged to Laurasia and Gondwana are now in very different positions.

Pangaea

All of the Earth's continents were pushed together into a supercontinent called Pangaea (pronounced *pan-jee-uh*) about 250 million years ago. It was possible for many kinds of prehistoric plants and animals to spread around to most of the different continents because of the continuous landmass. The Americas as we know them today did not exist. North America belonged to the northern part of the supercontinent (called Laurasia), along with Europe and Asia. South America belonged to the southern part of the supercontinent (called Gondwana), along with Africa, Australia and Antarctica.

North America and South America had extremely different climates around 280 million years ago. Most of North America and other Laurasian continents had a warm, rainy climate, covered with **tropical** swamps. At the same time, South America was positioned closer to the South Pole. South America and other Gondwanan continents had a colder, drier climate, and huge **glaciers** began to cover much of the landscape.

Break-up and isolation

By 200 million years ago, the plates below Pangaea were breaking it apart. Laurasia and Gondwana became two smaller supercontinents. Since Laurasia and Gondwana were separate landmasses, they could no longer share their wildlife so easily. By 150 million years ago, these two supercontinents were breaking up into the single continents we know today, including North America and South America. Although North America remained close to other continents, South America drifted completely away, and remained distant for millions of years.

Long ago, the Appalachian Mountains of North America connected with the mountains of Europe, when these two continents formed a continuous landmass.

Land bridges:
THE NARROW LINK

Today, few of the continents are closely connected. Most of them are entirely – or almost entirely – surrounded by water. Land connections between continents are mainly the narrow kind, such as an **isthmus**. Yet even narrow land bridges can make a big difference in the wildlife of a continent.

North American links

The great supercontinents of Laurasia and Gondwana began breaking up during the **Age of Reptiles,** around 200 million years ago. Most of the individual continents were separate by the beginning of the **Age of Mammals**, about 65 million years ago. Some continents still remained near others. For example, North America still lay near Europe and Asia. This made it possible for land connections to remain and ancient wildlife to migrate between these continents. Prehistoric cats, bears, horses, deer, tapirs, camels and elephants were some of the mammals that were shared by North America and Eurasia during this time.

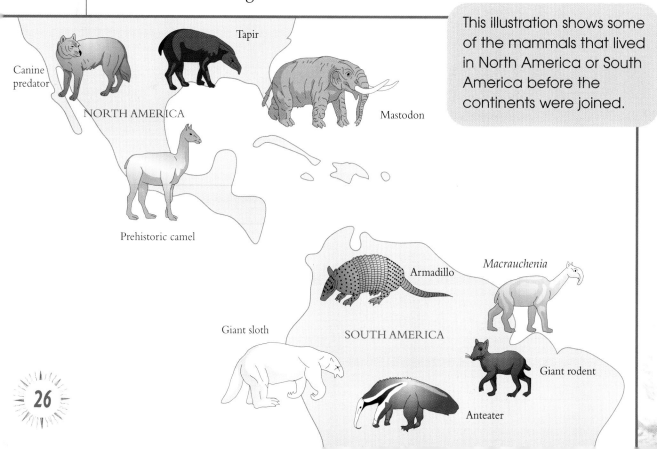

This illustration shows some of the mammals that lived in North America or South America before the continents were joined.

Tapir

Canine predator

NORTH AMERICA

Mastodon

Prehistoric camel

Armadillo

Macrauchenia

Giant sloth

SOUTH AMERICA

Giant rodent

Anteater

Isolation

Not all continents lay close to other continents during the Age of Mammals. South America became an 'island continent', surrounded by vast seas. Many of the animals that developed in South America at this time were found nowhere else in the world. These included mammals such as **sloths**, armadillos, giant anteaters and certain meat-eating **marsupials**. There were also many strange-looking mammals, completely unlike any living today, including a camel-like creature with a trunk like an elephant. These animals are now extinct.

Wildlife migrations

South America did not remain an island continent. Late in the Age of Mammals, the drifting plates below North America and South America began to bring these two continents closer together. Around three million years ago, the southern tip of North America touched the northern coast of South America, and a land bridge was formed which became the Isthmus of Panama. This enabled certain South American mammals to migrate into North America, including armadillos, anteaters, tree sloths and huge prehistoric ground sloths. The land bridge also enabled certain North American mammals – including cats, bears, deer, **tapirs** and the camel-like ancestors of llamas – to migrate into South America. The same land bridge would later be crossed by humans.

South American marsupials

More marsupials live in Australia than any other continent. Yet many prehistoric marsupials also lived in ancient South America. The largest of these South American marsupials were **predators**. One of them was as big as a tiger and had a pair of long, sabre-like fangs (similar to the sabre-toothed cats of ancient North America). There were also many kinds of **opossums**. Opossums still survive in many parts of North and South America.

Pumas, or cougars, are large cats that crossed the Isthmus of Panama and are now found throughout the Americas.

27

Land bridges:
DROPPING SEAS

In order to form a land bridge, two continents must be close to each other. But sometimes a land bridge also depends on other conditions, such as the level of the sea and the width of the continental shelf.

The continental shelf

A continent does not simply end where its land meets the sea. Beyond the shore lies a part of the seabed called the continental shelf, covered by shallow water, and it is considered part of the continent. The width of the continental shelf can vary a great deal. In some places it is very narrow; in other places it reaches out hundreds of kilometres. Beyond the continental shelf, a slanting surface called the continental slope leads down to the deep ocean floor.

Dropping seas

Sometimes the seas flood over the continents. This is likely to happen when the Earth's climate is very warm, causing the **polar icecaps** to melt and the seas to flood into low-lying areas of land. The continents have been flooded in this way many times over the past 500 million years.

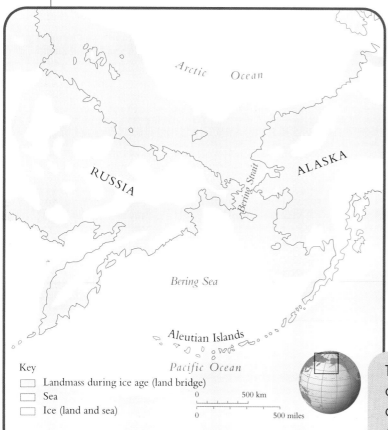

Arctic Ocean

RUSSIA

ALASKA

Bering Strait

Bering Sea

Aleutian Islands

Pacific Ocean

Key
- Landmass during ice age (land bridge)
- Sea
- Ice (land and sea)

0   500 km

0   500 miles

The seas were much lower during the last ice age, creating a land bridge between North America and Asia.

Yet at other times, the sea level drops and the continental shelves become exposed, increasing the land surface. This is likely to happen when the Earth's climate is much colder, causing icecaps to form again and the seas to retreat from low areas of land, and even from the continental shelves. This is what happened many thousands of years ago, during the last **ice age**. Where the exposed continental shelves reach out far enough to connect two different continents, they form a land bridge.

The Bering land bridge

The narrow part of the sea that lies between Asia and North America is called the Bering Strait. There is no deep ocean floor below the Bering Strait because it is the place where two continental shelves come together. By 15 000–30 000 years ago, the sea level had dropped far enough to turn this continuous continental shelf into dry land. The Bering Strait became the Bering land bridge. The first people to enter North America came from Asia across this land bridge. It probably took them a week to travel the distance (about 80 kilometres). By the end of the last ice age, around 10 000 years ago, the sea level rose once more and the Bering land bridge was again flooded to become the Bering Strait. By this time, people were already settled in the Americas.

Land bridges
across the world

The first humans lived in Africa. They crossed land bridges to spread throughout most of the continents. First they migrated into Asia and Europe, which formed a continuous **landmass** with Africa. When continental shelves were exposed during the last ice age, humans could cross the Bering land bridge from Asia into the Americas. They could also cross a similar land bridge from New Guinea (near Asia) to Australia. Antarctica was the only continent too remote to be reached by humans during the last ice age.

Navajo and Anasazi **petroglyphs** on the walls of Canyon de Chelly, Arizona, document prehistoric life in the canyon.

GLOSSARY

Age of Mammals a time in Earth's history when mammals became the largest animals (about 65 million years ago to recent times)

Age of Reptiles a time in Earth's history when reptiles became the largest animals (about 250–65 million years ago)

arid dry, with little or no water

capybaras large South American rodents, which can grow up to 1.2 metres long (the world's largest rodent)

cavy the name of several plant-eating rodents from South America. The guinea pig is an example of a cavy.

Christianity the Christian religion, based on the teachings of Jesus

conifers non-flowering trees or shrubs that bear cones. The leaves can have a needle, oval, scale or barbed shape.

crust the Earth's outermost layer of rock, about 8–70 kilometres thick

deciduous trees trees that shed their leaves during a certain time of the year, such as autumn

democracies societies governed by voting citizens, or by elected officials

domestic animals tame animals that are useful to humans

exposed laid open to sun, wind and rain

fertile rich in nutrients

glaciers masses of ice that move slowly across the land

ice age a time when parts of the Earth became colder and were covered by glaciers. There have been many ice ages in ancient history.

icecaps permanent coverings of ice

isthmus a narrow strip of land connecting two larger areas

Judaism the Jewish religion, based on the Torah (the Old Testament of the Bible); followers are called Jews

kinkajous slender, yellow-brown mammals that are members of the raccoon family

landmass a large area of land, such as a continent

manatees large water mammals, sometimes called sea cows, with flippers and a flat, oval tail

mantle the layer of very dense rock (about 2900 kilometres thick) below the Earth's crust

marsupials mammals that carry their young in a pouch

migrate to move from one area to another

military dictator a member of the armed forces who rules a country with complete power

nations   countries or kingdoms; the people within countries or kingdoms, with a common government

natural resources   supplies of useful materials from nature, such as soil, water or minerals

opossums   possums, especially those native to the Americas

peccaries   pig-like mammals of the Americas

petroglyphs   rock drawings or carvings made by people from long ago

polar   of the Arctic or Antarctic regions

predators   animals that hunt, kill and eat other animals

pronghorns   antelope-like mammals with horns and hooves

sloths   tree-living mammals of South and Central America

sorghum   a tall cereal plant used for feeding livestock or for making products like molasses and syrup

standard of living   the level of goods and income enjoyed by a society

tapirs   large, pig-like mammals related to the horse and rhinoceros

tectonic   relating to the structure and changes in the Earth's crust

temperate   moderate; not permanently hot or cold. Temperate climates are those with temperate characteristics, such as a Mediterranean or a cool temperate climate.

timber   trees or forested land; wood used for constructing buildings, furniture and wooden objects

tropical   of the tropics, the warm regions around the equator

Vikings   pirates, warriors and explorers from Scandinavia who invaded many parts of Europe from the 700s to the 900s

FURTHER INFORMATION

Websites

About Geography   **http://geography.about.com**
Includes sites for a world atlas and maps, glossary, quizzes and homework help.

National Geographic   **www.nationalgeographic.com**
Includes sites for travel, maps, news, nature, history and culture.

Books

Lands and Peoples. Grolier Incorporated, Danbury, 1995.

The Usborne-Internet-Linked Encyclopedia of World Geography. Usborne Publishing Ltd, London, 2001.

World Explorer series. Prentice Hall, Needham, 1998.

INDEX